Beside You

Supporting Your Dying Loved One

Kerry Arquette

Cover, interior design: Susan Malikowski, DesignLeaf Studio

Cover illustration: Pimchawee, Shutterstock, Susan Malikowski

This book is for my husband Mark Senn,
who is my everything.

The News

You will respond to the news that

your loved one is dying as

YOU

will respond to the news

that your loved one is dying.

Because no two people are the same.

We each have a unique and very personal
reaction to hearing that somebody we
love will no longer be a part of our
physical world.

Some people are overwhelmed with emotion,
while others shut down completely.

Dying (numb)

"Dying" . . . the word hovers . . .
The mist of breath carrying it
condenses and clots,
Darkening and becoming dense as a
cannon ball.
It drops to my feet.
The floor caves in.
I follow it down and down and down
and down . . .

The silence pads our landing in a vault
Where my inhale seems an offense.
Numb-brain. Eyes unfocused.
Unfeeling.
I will stay here until they call me back,
Demanding that I respond
to their news . . .
Demanding I feel when all I want is
To stay here in this well, in the dark,
And try to remember how to breathe.

Flood
of
Feelings

Dying (ROARING)

She said, "He's dying."

Disbelief. You don't know what you're talking about. He's fine! **Denial**. Besides, he would have told me if he was sick.

Guilt. Or . . . maybe he thought that he couldn't count on me. **Regret**. Now it's too late to do those things we planned. **Fear**. If he can die, then anybody can die!
I CAN DIE!

 Doubt. I don't know how to treat him now.

Anger. He knew that _____ was bad for him.

Blame. If the doctors really cared, they would save him! **Confusion #1**. Why won't he try experimental treatments?

Confusion #2. How could God have let this happen? **Hopelessness**. There's nothing I can do to stop this! **Sadness**. I want to cry enough tears to wash away the truth that

He's dying.

Types of Death

The way a person dies has an impact

on those around him and those left behind.

Types of death can be discussed in terms
of "Sudden and Unexpected,"

and

"Slow and Anticipated."

Sudden and Unexpected

Hearing about a loved one's sudden,

unexpected death is like being

SLAMMED

against a wall by an unknown assailant.

You didn't see it coming, couldn't prepare for it,

couldn't plan a defense!

One moment you are tra-la-la-ing along ,

and the next, you're in the gutter wailing.

Recovering from an unexpected death can

take a long time because you must first

come to the realization that he or she is truly

gone.

Accepting that isn't easy.

Out of the Blue

A METEOR HIT THE

EARTH YESTERDAY.

    OUT OF THE **7.674** BILLION

    HUMANS

    IN

    THE

    WORLD,

IT SLAMMED INTO SOMEONE I KNEW.

WHAT WERE THE CHANCES OF THAT?!!

NOW THEY ARE GONE, AND I AM

A PUDDLE OF **muck** ON THE SIDEWALK

THAT PEOPLE STEP AROUND,

AVERTING THEIR EYES.

THEY'LL NEED TO GET USED TO IT,

BECAUSE I'M GOING TO BE DOWN HERE

FOR A LONG, LONG TIME.

Slow and Anticipated

If you know a death is coming, you have

an opportunity to prepare for it.

You can be actively involved in helping

your relative or friend get ready and put

affairs in order.

And you can say your goodbyes.

However, the longer process of passing can be

exhausting

for both you and the dying.

Don't be ashamed if the thought,

"I just want this to be over!" crosses your mind.

IF IT DIDN'T,

YOU WOULDN'T BE HUMAN.

Life and Death
in Slow Motion

The bathroom faucet drips.
In you charge, armed with a wrench.
But, reaching the basin, you stop.
A waterdrop is poised at the tap's lip.
As you watch, it elongates into a tear.
The weight of the ballooning bottom
Stretches thin the upper portion,
Which clings to the spigot
like a tiny warrior,

.

The teardrop becomes an
exclamation point,
The water-heavy base yearning toward
The hard porcelain sink bowl below,
While the upper tether holds
to its mooring.

And then, it's over . . . .

. . . . The drop releases its grip on the tap,

Landing

—and then it's down the drain.

You realize the saga took

only a second or two.

But time is tricky.

A tick can feel like an hour,

And an ending...

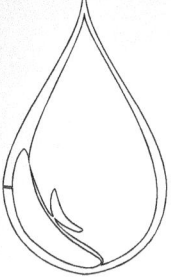

Like an eternity.

Your Role

If your loved one is in the process of dying, the type and amount of interaction you have with them and surrounding family will depend upon many things including your relationship with those involved, how close you live, your schedule, your personality, and your capacity to care-tend.

The idea of tending a dying person may seem terrifying—which makes sense. Things we're unfamiliar with almost always are. And (unless you are in the medical field), these days dying is something that's not even
talked about,

      let alone,

           witnessed.

Which is weird,
since it's all around us

or,

it **used** to be.

A Little
History Lesson

A hundred years ago in America most people died at home taken care of by their family. Because many households included multi-generations, there were a lot of people to help. Children were brought up watching and learning how to tend and nurture the ill and dying.

The lucky ones had a doctor in the area who would drop by with a medical bag (filled with very little because many of the tools, and medications that could cure illness and injury hadn't yet been invented). Most doctors focused on making patients comfortable rather than extending lives.

Things changed slowly and wars were largely responsible for propelling modern medical practices. For example, World War I introduced a greater use of blood transfusions. Then came World War II, which proved the effectiveness of antibiotics and expanded the success of orthopedic surgeries.

In America just after WW II, President Truman signed a bill, which supplied federal funds to build hospitals and clinics. And up they went, filled with the newest concepts and contraptions. Small town doctors saw the shining new facilities and said, "WOW!" So, they packed their doctor-bags and went to work at the big medical institutions, leaving many smaller communities without medical care.

Eventually people who lived in areas without doctors, as well as those in urban communities, all converged on hospitals and major medical centers for their care. Hospitals really **were** the place to be. They had all the newest research, medications, and technologies. Hospital doctors could induce labor, offer dialysis, perform microsurgery, image internal organs, and perform transplants.

Doctors who could do these amazing things were viewed by patients, and themselves, as nothing short of miracle workers...warriors against death (despite the fact that by the 1950s 61% of all deaths happened in hospitals.)

As doctors and nurses stepped up, families and loved ones were pushed back, away from the bedside of their loved ones.

Hospital regulations limited visitation time, and family was often instructed to call a nurse instead of trying to aid their loved one.

Little by little Americans were distanced from the dying process. Eventually, many adults could say that they had never seen anyone die. Dying and death became an unfamiliar and scary part of life, rather than a familiar and natural experience. And so, the ancient art of tending to the dying was lost.

Which is why you, most likely, do not believe that you know what to do at the bedside of somebody who is nearing death's door.

The truth is you probably know more than you realize. It is built into us.

We simply need to get back in touch with what it means to nurture selflessly.

Listen to the Voices

Deep, deep inside of me,
Another person resides.
She pokes me
With a sharp finger and says,
"Remember what you know.
You were not born new."
"You are the daughter of my daughter,
The son of my blood.
"My essence flows through your veins,
As yours now flows through mine.

"In this circle of life and death,
Nothing is lost or forgotten.
"You know how to ease suffering.
As have all who came before.

"You must simply quiet your mind
And listen to our heartbeats."

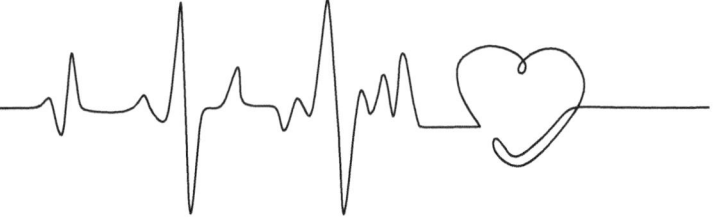

Visiting Your Dying Loved One

Dying is a solo experience.

Nobody can understand the sensations in a dying person's body or the depth of thoughts and feelings that fill their mind.

For a person who is dying, the things that once mattered are no longer imperative. A person who is dying has stepped out of the human rank and file.

You can't change the fact that your loved one must navigate the process solo, but solo doesn't mean alone.

Having somebody nearby can provide enormous comfort.

Tips for Visiting

- **Call before you visit** to make sure your loved one is up for a visit.

- **Consider taking another person** who also knows the dying so you two can chat while your loved one listens and rests.

- **Don't stand over the bed**. Take a seat nearby. Speak clearly and slowly.

- **Hold a hand**. Share a gentle hug. Touch is a way to say, "I care."

- **Your friend or relative is the same person** as before. Treat him or her as you always have.

- **Pick up on cues—if your loved one's eyes keep wandering** to the tv, be quiet and watch the program.

- **Remember that sitting** with the dying doesn't have to be somber. If you find something funny, chances are so do they. LAUGH!

Bearing Gifts

A gift is a way to say, "I love you," but somebody who is dying truly doesn't need more "stuff." So, think about giving something that can be enjoyed now.

What you bring depends somewhat on the state of the person being visited. What can they do? What will they enjoy?

You may wish to expand your gifting to include the caregivers of your dying loved one. They are working hard, and acknowledging their efforts will be truly valued.

Stuff

We **work** to earn money

To buy things

That give us pleasure.

More things,

More pleasure.

We work to earn money.

Dying, we must leave behind,

The bought things,

And cling only to

That which can pass

With us thru the veil...

Memories, Faith, and Love.

Gift Ideas

What you bring should be meaningful in the present. Ways to share good memories, and things that provide immediate pleasure and comfort are good choices.

- **A digital photo** frame loaded with pictures
- **Letters** from friends
- **Books** on tape
- **Candy** or other favorite edibles
- **Lotions**
- **Gift cards** for manicures or facials with practitioners who make house visits
- **A journal** or digital recorder
- **A super cozy** blanket
- **Homemade soup** or another favorite dish
- **A small laptop** computer such as an IPad

- **Books of crossword** puzzles or sudoku

- **A song** or piece of art that you have created

- **A pet visit**

- **A visit or telephone call** from a very dear friend who lives far away

- **A playlist** of songs from their best-time years

IOUs To . . .

- **Drive them** to doctor appointments

- **Do the laundry**

- **Mow** the lawn

- **Walk the dog** or offer to take it to the vet or to a grooming appointment

- **Grocery** shop

- **Pick up** prescriptions

- **Help declutter** drawers, cabinets, closets

What To Expect When Visiting

Your loved one is going through enormous changes, both physically and emotionally. All of this is a normal part of the process. Be as open as possible and ready to take it in stride. Knowing what you might experience can help prepare you.

Odor

As a person nears death, metabolism changes can create unusual and sometimes unpleasant smells. Medications can also affect smells, as can the undergarments used when a dying person loses the ability to use the toilet.

Come Prepared

If you are highly affected by odors consider the following:

- **Bring a gift** of a scented candle and light it.

- **Bring essential oils** to apply to your loved one.

- **Bring a gift of lavender**, jasmine, lily, chamomile, or geranium potpourri.

- **Open a window** if the weather is nice.

- **Stand back** a distance from the dying.

- **Put coffee grounds** in the room.

- **Apply a vapor rub** under your nose or pop a vapor lozenge in your mouth.

- **Chew strongly flavored** mint gum.

Breathing

Those who are nearing death often have trouble breathing either because of illness, medication, or because their lungs are having to work harder to compensate for the rest of the body.

The "death rattle" you may have heard about is just phlegm in the back of the throat, which the dying can't clear.

It doesn't hurt your loved one.

I'd Breathe For You

If there was a way to do it,
I'd breathe for you.
I'd open the window and take
Huge gulps of air and then carry them
to your lips.

I would will your ribcage
To float and **descend**
As effortlessly as a sleeping child's.

I would breathe next to you quietly,
My inhale a microsecond
Before yours . . . to clear a path,
So you would not have
To work so hard.

Temperature Control

The dying may be tossing off the blankets because it's too hot one minute and icy the next. It's the body's inability to adjust to temperature.

Fatigue and Sleepiness

The dying sleep. A LOT. If you arrive for a visit and find your friend or family member sleeping, don't try to wake them. Just sit quietly nearby.

Irritability

Your loved one may seem angry. And why not? It seems unfair that they have to leave behind everyone and everything and accept declining health while others are running laps at the park.

Distraction

If you feel that the person you are visiting seems unfocused, you are probably right. Medications can blur the mind, and pain, fear, and exhaustion make it hard to be socially attentive. And . . . let's face it—this person has got a lot going on.

Joy

Just seeing you may be enough to rouse your loved one from a cocoon of blankets. Your face may be what's needed to light up your loved one's heart.

Love has **always been,**

is, and **always will be** important.

Maybe never more so than when we are dying.

Let's Talk About Talk

So, you've entered the room of your dying friend or relative and aren't sure what to say.

It feels **more than important** that you get this right.

You don't want to say the wrong thing because you're afraid it will make things worse.

On the other hand, time is counting down and opportunities to talk are short.

It can feel like you are caught
in a damned-if-you-do,
and damned-if-you-don't situation!

Noise

When I get nervous, I babble.
I talk on and on about this and that,
None of which matters...
I just can't shut off the words
That gush out of my mouth,
Like water from a firehose.

When I get nervous, I can't say anything,
Because I can't think of anything to say.
I make weird sounds, clear my throat,
Cough, and click my nails together.
I open and close my mouth like a guppy.

When I get nervous I over-share,
Tell stupid jokes, laugh too loud,
Express opinions on things
I know nothing about,
Wade into topics that should be left alone.
I'm so obnoxious

I don't want to be with me.

When I'm nervous I forget that
conversation is like music.
It has natural ebbs and flows...
A crescendo and then a beat or two
or three where nothing happens.
When I'm nervous,
I forget that not all music
must have lyrics.

The Nitty Gritty
of Conversation

Here are some loose guidelines involving conversation when visiting the room of a dying loved one.

FIRST,

let's look at some of the things that might come out of your mouth that would have been better if you
CHEWED them and SWALLOWED.

NOT So Great

- **You're looking great!** (Dying people know they look awful.)

- **You're going to beat this thing.** (Chances aren't good,and they know it.)

- **Everything happens for a reason.** (So, they're suffering for a reason?)

- **It could be worse.** (really?!)

  I had an aunt/uncle/cousin who had this and lived to 90! (Good for them!)

- **How are you?** (The answer is obvious.)

- **I'm sorry you're dying.** (unless your loved one brings it up, don't wash his or her face in the inevitable.)

- **Wait a minute** . . . I have to take this phone call/return this text. (Nothing is more important than the person in front of you.)

- **You're going home to God!** (Unless your loved one has professed this belief and you are lovingly reinforcing it.)

Better

- **How are you feeling** today?

- **Are you up for a visitor** or would you rather I come another time?

- **Please tell me when** you want me to leave.
  I mean it!

- **Do you remember when** you and I....!?

- **I've always meant** to thank you for...

- **What can I do** to make you more comfortable?

- **Is there anything** you'd like me to do for your family?

- **Is there anything** you'd like to talk about?

- **What would you like** me to bring you??

OF COURSE

I'LL COME BACK!

Best

I love you !

Conversation NO! NOs!

Nope #1

This is probably a good time to state that, no matter how good your intentions, using the platform of dying to evangelize is just plain wrong, UNLESS your loved one has asked you to discuss your beliefs with them.

Nope #2

Do not try to talk your friend or family member out of the decisions he or she has made concerning treatment or lack of treatment.

THIS IS YOUR LOVED ONE'S DEATH, NOT YOURS. RESPECT HOW IT'S BEEN ENVISIONED.

Nope #3

This is not the time to share your grievances. It might make you feel good to get them off your chest but will add pain and stress to the dying.

Nope #4

If you need to confess, find a priest, or write down your indiscretions in a journal. Do not dump them on your dying loved one who has no use for the information.

Not Necessary

I don't have to be clever.

I don't have to be wise.

I don't have to be entertaining.

I don't have to be uplifting.

I don't have to be a cheerleader.

I don't have to downplay the situation.

I don't have to pretend —

And that means you don't have to pretend.

I don't have to be anything but me,

Right here, in this moment.

And you can be you.

Human ~~DOING~~

Human BEING

How to Be

Now you have some idea about what to say and what not to say. That's a good starting point.

But what do you DO when you are with one who is dying? You can't just sit and stare as if waiting for a last breath.

But you can just sit.

Don't Want To

I want to be anywhere but here . . .

Like . . .

Getting my teeth drilled,
Cross-country-tripping in August
In a car with broken air conditioning,
Shopping for a bathing suit under cruel lights,
Changing the cat litter box,
Searching for the lone lost sock,
Cleaning the bathroom toilet . . .

I'd like to be anywhere but here,
With somebody I love who is dying,
And yet, there is nowhere else I can be
When our time together is so short.

So, I sit.

Here.

Your Role
in the Death

The role you play in the period before death depends on many things. Only you can determine if you are willing and able to be part of the inner circle of carers.

A commitment to shepherd or walk the final path alongside a dying person can be exhausting. It can also be one of the most rewarding and life-changing acts you may ever do.

Hands

I signed on a dotted line
With a hand that held no pen,
But held your hand in mine.

I made a solemn pledge
To hold that hand and
Walk with you to life's edge.

Then unclasp our hands—
A kiss, to see you off
To unknown lands.

What To DO While Attending?

You have thought it through and decided that you want to walk this last journey by your dying friend or relative. But **what does that mean** exactly? What can you do to help?

The Together Gift

Let's look at photos
Together,
Or watch TV
Together
Or pet the cat
Together
Or listen to music
Together.

What we do
Doesn't really matter
As long as we are
Together.

Hold Space

Holding Space is a term used by many who work with those experiencing deep emotions. It means being completely present EMOTIONALLY, PHYSICALLY, AND MENTALLY.

When holding space, you create an environment in which your loved one feels totally accepted, supported, and able to expose deep personal thoughts and feelings. You withhold judgment, ego, and opinions. What you think and feel is unimportant.

THE PERSON IN CRISIS

IS THE

ONLY

PERSON

THAT MATTERS.

I Am Here With All My Heart

I am privileged to be in the audience
Of this Final Act
of a one-of-a-kind story.
I hold my breath,
sitting on the edge of my seat,
While it is played out to
the last word and sigh.
I have nothing to offer
the plot or the star.

I am not here to edit or critique.

I sit outside the spotlight.

I watch.

I listen.

I allow myself
to be caught up in the narrative.
My heart lifts and plummets
as the words tumble
From the lips of my
dying
loved one.
And inwardly
I applaud
the courage it takes
To share life's stories while the curtain

falls.

Offer Physical Comfort

Unless you are a medical professional or have been trained to perform medical tasks, leave those to the doctors, nurses, and aids. There are other ways to show you care.

You might, for example,

- **Comb your loved** one's hair, file nails
- **Perform gentle hand** or foot massages
- **Apply lotion** or lip balm
- **Offer sips of water** or ice chips
- **Change a soiled** pillowcase
- **Fetch an extra blanket** or remove an unneeded one
- **Open or close** windows.

The Little
and
Big Things

Here is a balm
for your chapped skin...

I'm here...
hoping that
I can serve as a
balm for your heart.

Help Complete What is Important

Ask if your loved one has unfinished business he or she would like help completing. There may also be things that don't fall in the "business" category that you could help complete LIKE...

- **Taking a car trip** to see Mount Rushmore

- **Knitting and pearling** that half-finished sweater

- **Eating a favorite meal** and having TWO desserts

- **Corresponding with** a long-lost friend

- **Attending church** services

- **Fiinishing reading** MOBY DICK.

Keep In Mind

The dying process is often unpredictable. It can take more or less time than you think. If the unfinished task is important, prioritize it!!!

Wrapping up
the "wants"
of your loved one
can create a sense
of completeness
to life.

This is the Time

There will be time for resting later.
But now is a chance for stringing
Final pearls on the necklace
That you will wear to celebrate
Your well-lived life.

Now is the time for

D A N C I N G

last steps, And

painting

final strokes, For

writing

odes to yourself,

And reading them to found people
You lost somewhere along the way.

This is a time for exploring mysteries
You hadn't time or interest in before...
To ask,

"How, when, why, where?"

To gasp in wonder
And laugh
as you roll around in your old fears.

Here is a pearl,
and another,
Plucked from the oysters of your life,

Just waiting for you . . .

Just waiting for this moment . . .

For you to stop

and be **awed** by their beauty.

Explore Faith

The time before death often ignites thoughts about mortality and whether there is or isn't a supreme being or an afterlife. Your loved one may wish to talk about spiritual views on dying. At this stage, the last thing you should do is rock the dying's spiritual boat, leaving him with less comforting conviction.

If you are uncertain how to navigate this topic, ask if you can bring in books or lectures that might be important and provide information or perspective valuable to the conversation. Offer to read passages from religious texts that may bring comfort. Many religious leaders will make house calls. Ask whether you should set up a visit.

Supporting Faith

If your loved one is spiritual or religious, ask whether you could bring items that might be comforting

- **Prayer beads** and metals with spiritual images or verses

- **Religious candles** showing the images of saints, or abundance candles

- **A crucifix, Star of David**, Buddhist lotus flower, endless knot, Hindu Om, or prayer flags etc. (Research symbols before arriving with your hands full.)

- **Holy books, tapes**, and images

- **Tapestries that evoke** a sense of spiritual connection

- **An altar** (make one out of stacked cigar boxes sold in hobby stores.) Decorate the boxes with thoughts and sayings that resonate with your loved one.

- **Religious** or spiritual music

Psychological Needs

Your loved one may have overflowing emotions. Be prepared to turn off the TV or computer and listen actively, or simply hold space (as discussed earlier),

OR

Your loved one may be interested in an interactive and dynamic conversation. The things he or she wants to talk about could make you frightened or uncomfortable. You may not know how to contribute. There are therapists who specialize in death and dying. If you are out of your depth, call them for help.

Drowning
in Feelings

Hold on to me
If your emotions are so
Heavy that you feel pulled under.
Together we can
Kick,
Splash, stroke,
And doggy paddle
our way to the edge,
Where we can crawl out of the mire
And catch our breath.

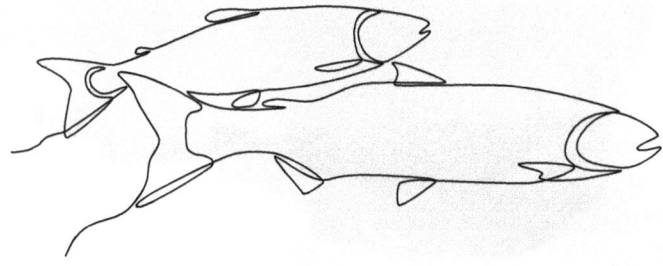

Celebrating Your Loved One's Life

If you have a span of time prior to the death of your friend or relative, consider the many ways you can celebrate his or her life.

When life ahead is short, the past becomes even more important. Talking about personal history helps the dying realize how rich and remarkable their life has been. They may come to understand that there is no need to write another life chapter, but a need to come up with an absolutely AWESOME ending to their story.

A Life Review

A life review allows your loved one to rewalk the path he or she has trod by recounting memories.

You may wish to record or write down the stories for future generations. Your role is to help the memories flow.

You may feel more comfortable with a prepared list of predetermined questions, but use it only if the conversation is faltering.

If you do need to supply prompts, you can't go wrong keeping in mind the journalist's mantra: Who? What? When? Where? Why? How?

There are examples on the next pages!

Who

Who was with you? Who do you wish was there?
Who did or said what and when? Who changed
because it happened, and how?

What

What do you remember about _____? What
was it like? What did you do then? What were
you thinking? What were you feeling? What would
you change if you could do it all over again?
What are you proudest of doing? What are you
proudest of accomplishing?

When

When did it happen? When did you react,
and how? When did you see it as important?
When did you wish you'd done something
else? When did you feel your most _____?

When did you first experience love/envy/
jealousy/God, etc.?

Where

Where did it take place? Where were others? Where
did you go and where did you go after that? Where
do you wish you'd been instead? Where was _____?

Why

Why did you make the choice/choices you made?
Why did you decide not to _____? Why did it
matter? Why does that event stand out in your
memory? Why is it important to talk about it now?
Why don't you want to talk about it?

How

How did it happen? How did it end? How did you
feel? How did it impact your life? How did it impact
the lives of others?

Review Tips

- **Tape or record** the interview instead of taking notes. Note-taking makes conversations less spontaneous and can intimidate a speaker.

- When appropriate, **ask what your loved one remembers** about smells, sounds, tastes, colors, the weather, what people were wearing, textures of things touched. His memories will paint a rich picture and make the events more vivid.

- **Don't feel the need to fill silences**. A long pause is often followed by more talk. Allow your loved one the space to think about what to say next.

- **Focus on the storyteller**. Do not interrupt. *LEAN* INTO the narrative.

- **While you may wish** to create a list of questions you'd like answered, go with the flow. Only revert to the list when you have thoroughly explored the subject at hand.

Interview Preparations

- **Have a glass of water available** for your loved one. Be attuned to whether the story-teller is becoming tired. When that happens, stop the session, and continue later.

- **Participating in a life review** will take more of an effort the closer your friend or family member comes to death, so don't leave it half-done.

- **Set a day and time** to continue with the review. This makes it clear that the hard work that your loved one is doing is important—important enough to prioritize.

Letter Memorials

Invite friends from throughout your loved one's life to write down their memories about times they have shared.

Encourage the letter-writers to include photos, if they have them. Read the letters to your dying friend or relative during visits. Share them with others at end-of-life events and, perhaps, at the memorial service.

Letter to My Dad

I'll never forget that time when . . .
A ram chased you at the Living History Museum

But you vaulted a fence into an empty pen.
You slipped and sat down in muck and mud,
And were still sitting when the ram remembered
   how he had gotten out of that pen in the
   first place.
You proved your fence-jumping skills twice
   that day!

                        I am still laughing.

Living Funeral

The concept of a living funeral is gaining momentum across America, driven by the idea that it is a shame for the dying to miss out on hearing the thoughts and memories of those who might speak at their funeral or memorial service.

So, family and friends are throwing pre-death parties to honor their dying loved ones. Living funerals can be small or large, formal, or less so.

The only "must" is that the occasion should be held while your loved one can still enjoy it. A social gathering may be too exhausting for a person who is farther along in the dying process.

Planning the Living Funeral

- **Consult with the person** being honored when creating the guest list.

- **Include favorite foods** of the dying or foods that hold a special meaning.

- **Make sure you have a special chair** set aside for your loved one and several chairs nearby for those who wish to sit and talk.

- **Put together, or hire somebody** who can create, a slide show featuring photos of the guest of honor that span the decades, and include people who have played meaningful roles.

- **Display** the memorial letters.

- **Put a plastic sheet** under a white tablecloth. Scatter fabric markers across the cloth. Invite attendees to write memories or thoughts on the cloth and sign and

date them. Wash the cloth with a cup of vinegar
to set the ink.

· **Invite a designated number** of people to offer toasts.

MORE Living Funeral

· **Ask those who can't attend** to video themselves
sharing their thoughts and memories. Play them
at the party.

· **Include music** that is meaningful to your loved one.

· **Make time** for the honoree to speak, if desired.

· **Keep an eye on** your loved one who may tire easily.
Call a stop to the festivities as soon as you see that
happening.

Ethical Will

Ask if your dying friend or relative would like to
create an ethical will. These wills provide a way

for the creator to share life lessons. This is an opportunity to hand along **wisdom**, and detail **wishes** and **expectations** for familial generations to come.

Journals
or Scrapbooks

Create journals by copying important memorabilia—such as photos, birth certificates, school report cards, post cards from travels, marriage certificates, awards, letters, and cards.

To prevent items from yellowing and cracking, invest in journals or scrapbooks that have acid and lignin-free pages and that do not contain PVC. Make multiple copies of the books and hand them out as gifts for close relatives.

Launch a Scholarship

Setting up a memorial scholarship fund to further the lives of future generations is a wonderful way for the memory of your loved one to live on.

Create an evergreen donation, or a series of donations, to a cause close to your loved one's heart.

Never Forgotten

Bodies were not made
   for "forever."
They are on loan—
Walking, talking,
   tiny houses,
That we try to maintain
   as best we can.
But eventually,
   inevitably,
Another shingle
   or layer of paint,
A knee replacement
   or miracle pill,
Cannot fool
   Father Time,
Who recognizes that
   a patch-job is
   just a patch job.

It's time for something
   new to rise
From the foundation
   of our faltering
   abodes
   . . . the next
   generation.
But we will never be
   forgotten because
   somewhere,
   just below,
A grain of sand
   is left behind,
   Sloughed
From the cornerstone
   of our lives,
Proving that we were
   here.

Gifting of Meaningful Possessions

You might think that it would be uncomfortable for your dying friend or relative to give away important possessions while still alive, but many people enjoy the act of bestowing gifts—placing treasures in the hands of new owners and watching their faces light up.

This gifting provides an opportunity for the stories behind the items to be shared, which makes them that much more precious. Take photos of each gifted item and record its story to include in an album.

Repurpose Possessions

Finding new uses for your loved one's special

possessions is a creative way to honor them.

- **Turn old T-shirts** into a quilt.

- **Turn well-loved clothing** or linens into pillows for ring bearers.

- **Pull apart inexpensive jewelry** to embellish scrap book pages.

- **Turn unique buttons** into memorial jewelry.

- **Copy favorite life photos**, cut the images into strips and weave together your loved one's life.

- **Use a blow torch** (if you know how to use one safely or ask for help from a handy friend) to bend engraved silver spoons into bracelets.

- **Sew lacy handkerchiefs** into a meaningful baby quilt for a grandchild or great grandchild.

- **Collect your loved one's baby cups**, fill them with sand, and use them as holders for candles or as a Chanukah menorah.

- **Use demitasse cups** as Christmas tree ornaments.

Legal Matters

With the winds of emotion buffeting you, it can seem difficult to focus on the prosaic matters that must be dealt with prior to the death of a loved one. Here is a list of things that should be addressed.

Last Will and Testament

A legal document that outlines what to do with possessions, finances, and some responsibilities such as custody of children and pets.

Power of Attorney

A legal document in which the creator names who should look out for his or her best interests if he or she is incapacitated. There are various forms of power of attorney, and each plays a distinct role.

Living Will

A written statement detailing the desires of the

creator regarding medical treatment if they can not speak for themselves.

Medical Power of Attorney

A document that names a person trusted by the creator to make medical decisions that serve the dying's best interest if the dying can't speak. This document is important if a living will doesn't exist or is being questioned.

HIPPA Release

A release form that must be signed by the dying in order to allow specific people to have access to their medical records.

Letter of Intent

A non-legally binding document in which the creator spells out wishes when it comes to funeral arrangements, personal items not mentioned in the will, and statements of wishes and hopes for survivors.

Other Things to Consider

The last thing you want to undertake after the death of a loved one is a hunt for important information and documentation. While your friend or relative is still able to direct you, pull together the following:

You'll Be Glad You Did This!!!

- **Name and contact** information of lawyers
- **Name of bank**, banker, and bank account numbers
- **Access to safety deposit box**
- **Name of insurance company** and policy information
- **Name of investment firms** and details about investments
- **Liabilities**/what is owed to whom

- **Life insurance** policy

- **Pet's veterinarian**

- **Social security** information

- **Names and addresses** of close family members
  and friends

- **Location of birth**, death, divorce, citizenship, adoption,
  and other certificates

- **Names and information for religious** contacts

- **Organizations**, clubs, and other groups that should
  be informed of death

- **Mortgages** and debts

- **Credit card** names and numbers

- **Deed of trust** or mortgage for home/property

- **Most recent tax return** and accountant name

- **Car title and registration**

- **Passwords** for email and other accounts

The End
Draws Near

Before your loved one is too ill or weak to consider his or her options, there are things that need to be discussed. For some, these conversations are uncomfortable. For others, they are simply a matter of housekeeping . . . chores that must be addressed because there is no getting around them.

Time's Running Out

"I'll deal with that later,"

Takes on a new meaning,

When "later," has to be sooner.

And the "sooners" are

ticking down...

A clock with
a lost key.

"Traditional Burial"

The type of burial with which most people are familiar involves preparation of the body by a funeral home and internment in a cemetery. Sometimes the body is embalmed, but in most cases, embalming is not required by law. Embalming involves the removal of blood and the replacement with embalming fluid. Organs are filled with embalming fluid.

In a traditional funeral there is often a service. Viewing of the body may be an option. Then the body is transported to a grave site and is buried.

Dust to Dust

The seed snuggles, warm and protected.

Arms and legs, hands and feet grow
   like shoots.

Nourished, rocked and, when finally ready,

We spring forth and for the first time

Can see the infinity of the domed sky.

We crawl in green grasses,

Splash in blue waters, and run
   across golden fields.

A lifetime goes by.

Legs no longer run but stroll through fields
   under blue-water skies.

Then a day comes when,

Warm and protected,

We snuggle, safe in Earth's soil.

Cremation by Fire

Cremation by fire takes two to four hours. It involves putting a body into a chamber that is heated to between 1,400 and 1,800 degrees. The high heat reduces the body to bones, which are ground. The remains are returned to the family. They can either keep them or release them in a meaningful way such as scattered in a special place or freed into the wind in a secluded spot.

Prior to cremation a body may be displayed for family and friends and a service can be conducted.

Flying

I dreamed of flying when I was young,
Racing around the schoolyard swinging
A long, plastic beaded necklace
Above my head like rotor blades.
I believed that enough speed and determination
And perhaps a launch pad like the lip of a slide
Could wrench me free of gravity,
To swoop about the heads of classmates,
Who watched me soar,
Begging for rides.
Many years later, when I died,
They freed my ashes into the wind

AND FLYING WAS JUST AS WONDERFUL

AS I'D DREAMED IT MIGHT BE.

Newer Methods of Body Disposition

There is a movement afoot to offer a much wider list of options that are available in some areas of the country for the final disposition of a body.

Alkaline Hydrolysis/ Aqua Cremation/ Water Cremation

In this type of cremation, the body is put in a vat filled with gently agitated warm water and alkali. After several hours the body is reduced to bones, which are often ground and can be returned to the family. In some cases, the fluid, which is high in nutrients but devoid of DNA, can be used for fertilizing gardens.

At the time this book was published Alkaline Hydrolysis was legal in 19 states. Organic reduction/human composting was legal in even fewer.

Natural/Green Burial

In a natural/green burial, the body is buried in a simple shroud or biodegradable box. The body can be laid to rest in cemeteries offering special sections dedicated to green burials, cemeteries that do exclusively green burials, or conservation burial grounds.

Natural/green burial does not involve embalming, so the body must be preserved between death and burial by family at home or in a mortuary.

Natural Organic Reduction/ Human Recomposing

Recomposing of unembalmed human bodies involves putting a body inside a container and surrounding it with straw, grass, alfalfa, and other elements that reduce the body to soil in about thirty days. Any remaining bones are ground and may be sprinkled or buried.

Rites and Ceremonies

After-death ceremonies allow those left behind to commemorate the life of their loved one. These ceremonies can take many forms, from solemn to upbeat. Sometimes they are both.

Traditional Western Ceremony

Many who opt for a more traditional way of saying goodbye will include some, or all, of these options:

Wake

A wake is a gathering of loved ones. The body may or may not be present. The wake is a time to offer prayers and support for the living who are grieving.

Body Viewing

In a traditional funeral the body is most often

placed in a coffin and may be displayed for viewing to family and friends.

Service

After the viewing family may have a service (either at the mortuary or a church, etc.) The body is conveyed by the mortuary to its resting place in a conventional cemetery.

At the Cemetery

At the cemetery the coffin is lowered into a burial vault (sometimes called a liner) and sealed before being covered with earth. A second grave-side service may be performed at this time.

Direct Burial or Direct Cremation

If a family wishes their loved one to be buried or cremated, but does not wish to have a viewing, or formal service at that time, they may choose to have a ceremony or celebration at a later date.

Home Funeral

Home funerals are legal in all fifty states, although each state has laws governing the preservation of the body prior to disposal.

Some families choose to have a home funeral because they feel comforted that their loved one's body is in a familiar place rather than displayed in a less personal venue. During the process of home funerals, those closest to the deceased can

wash, anoint, clothe, adorn,

and sit with the body. In a home setting loved ones find privacy to mourn and to conduct religious observations and private rituals. The body is then transported to its final resting place.

Hands

Yours were the hands that cradled me and
Bathed my plump body in the kitchen sink.
Your hands
   bandaged my knees when I fell on the
   playground.
Your hands
   did their best to pin my short hair into
   a ballerina bun for my recitals.
Your hands
   pulled me tight into you before releasing
   me to start my own new life.
You used your hands to show me what love
   looked like.
And now, I will use mine to show YOU . . .

I understood the lessons.

Memorial Service and Life Celebration

A memorial service differs from a more traditional service because the body is often not present. For this reason, the gathering can be performed anywhere and at any time, from days to weeks, or even years after the death.

This is an opportunity for those who loved the deceased to gather to share stories. Food and drink may be a part of the gathering. If there are ashes to spread, this is a meaningful time to do so.

What Have You Been Waiting For?!!!

Honestly!

Do you think I've nothing better to do than
   wait around

While you plan this Life Celebration?!!

And I'm still waiting while you

heat up those little quiches from Costco,

And the green chili tamales from Costco,

And the creamy artichoke cheese dip from Costco,

And the sliced-and portioned
   cold cuts from Costco,

And the frozen shrimp from Costco,

And the bite-sized potato puffs from Costco,

And the pre-cooked pulled pork from Costco,

And the deviled eggs with just the right amount
   of mustard that you made from the hard boiled
   and peeled eggs you got from Costco?

You think I've got NOTHING BETTER TO DO
   than wait while you enjoy yourselves?!!!!!!!

Uhhh . . . okay . . . maybe you're right . . .

Humanist Funeral

When the deceased did not subscribe to religion, his or her loved ones may decide to have a funeral that focuses less on what happens in the here-after and more on the life of the deceased.

These funerals can be organized by friends or family, or they may hire the services of a celebrant, who is trained to organize and officiate at many types of funerals and celebrations.

My Vision

THE WORLD IS SPLENDER

It filled me and spilled from me.

I did not feel a need to label its source,

And yet was thankful for every

Taste, sensation, and sound.

Gratitude and love were my beacons.

Gratitude and love will follow me

Wherever I go or don't go.

Gratitude and love are everything

And gratitude and love

are enough.

Other Rites
and Celebrations

Every religion and many cultures have distinct ways own of honoring their dead. The previous pages focused broadly on what might be practiced across many Christian religions and throughout western cultures but in no way represent the customs of all religions, cultures, and peoples. These rites and celebrations are performed by the other four largest religions in the world.

Note that within each, there are many variations, and this information is a broad-brush attempt to inform based upon traditional practices.

Buddhist Wakes and Funerals

Depending upon the family, Buddhist wakes and

funerals are often simple ceremonies. A picture of the deceased sits in front of the casket and fruits, flowers, and candles may be present. A picture of Buddha will also be displayed. A monk may perform a ceremony. These rites can take place in a home, funeral home, or Buddhist temple.

Judaism

Traditionally, when somebody of the Jewish faith dies, the body is washed and then guarded around the clock until buried, which happens within 24 hours after death. Prior to the funeral, family members either rip their clothing or pin on a black ribbon. (This may also be done by a rabbi.) After the burial the family sits Shiva for seven days in mourning.

Hinduism Wakes and Funerals

When a practicing Hindu dies, there is usually a wake in the family's home. The wake is followed by a cremation ceremony. Between the 11th and the 31st day following the death the male mourners perform a ceremony believed to nourish and protect the soul as it proceeds to higher realms and, eventually on to reincarnation.

Islam

In the Islamic faith, burial is performed as quickly as possible after death. The body is washed and draped before being transported to the mosque. There, the Imam offers prayers. Men stand in front and women and children stand in the back. The body is taken for burial which, traditionally, is attended only by men. Each attendee throws three handfuls of dirt into the grave. After the burial mourners often gather at a family home to eat, talk, and begin a 40-day mourning period.

If you don't know, ASK

What should I wear, what should I bring, how early should I arrive? Should I take off my shoes? Should I bring something? Are there colors that are appropriate and others that are not? Do I participate or is that only for those who share the faith? How do I greet elders? Are there things I might do that are disrespectful? Can I bring someone? Will there be a reception? How long will it be? How do I know when I'm supposed to leave? Is there anything I can do to help? Will there be foods I can't eat? Are there follow-up events I should know about? How do I say, "I'm so sorry" in their language?

The Last Chapter

It is your friend's or relative's death, and he or she should be the one who determines what it looks like.

The thing is that most people have no concept that there are options other than the ones they see in movies . . .

THE DYING LIES IN BED WITH
A FEW WEEPING PEOPLE NEARBY,
WAITING FOR THE
L A S T   B R E A T H .

In truth, there are as many scenarios as there are humans. Exploring them starts with a conversation.

Given time and consideration, conversations that

begin with "I want to be surrounded by my loved ones," often evolve. You can help that happen by gently exploring themes and asking your loved one questions.

- **Where** do you want to die?

- **Whom** do you want present? Whom don't you want present?

- **Are there items you want** nearby like photos or meaningful possessions?

- **Are there prayers**, poems, or passages you'd like to be read?

- **Can we play music** that makes you feel peaceful?

- **Is there anything** that will make you uncomfortable?

The Conversation Develops...

As you continue to explore possibilities you may hear:

"I want the **windows open** if the weather allows."

"I don't want flowers (or) I only want **roses** in the room."

"I want **tables set up with puzzles and games**, so visitors have something to do."

"I want all my **photo albums** nearby so we can reminisce."

"I want an **open bar and good food** catered for visitors 24/7."

"There need to be enough **outlets for visitors** to charge their devices."

"I want **clean hair and I want my nails painted OPI's—I'm Really an Actress.**"

"I want **medical marijuana** from the dispensary on Central Blvd. Gummies."

"If people insist on crying, **I want them to leave the room to do it**."

"**No stinky candles!** And visitors shouldn't wear perfume or aftershave."

"**Red is my favorite color.** I'd like visitors to wear it."

"I want **new sheets on my bed daily**. New. Not just clean."

"I'd like to have all of the **Audrey Hepburn DVDs** available."

"**Clear** the room of **unnecessary knickknacks**."

"I want all the **cats in the room**. Even better...**ON the bed**!"

"**I want the curtains open during the day**. The more natural light the better."

"I don't want to die in bed. **I want to die in my recliner**."

Channel Bob Fosse

Your job is to choreograph the ending, bringing it as close to your loved one's vision as possible.

Remember, you don't need to do it alone. By allowing others to help, you are gifting them with the opportunity to show that they care.

Aid in Dying

In many cases the dying can be made comfortable with pain, anxiety, and other medications. In some cases, however, a loved one may wish to hurry the process of passing.

In all states, as of the publication of this book, a competent person may voluntarily end his or her life by refusing to eat or drink (Voluntarily Stopping Eating and Drinking—VSED).

Death may take days to weeks. Medical Aid in Dying (MAiD), also known as Physician-Assisted Dying (PAD) is currently legal in a handful of states. It involves a terminally ill qualifying and mentally-capable person ending life by taking medications prescribed by a physician and self-administered. Your loved one can learn more about this option by talking to their doctor.

When is Enough Enough?

Help IS Available

Caring for the dying is all-consuming. BEFORE YOU HIT YOUR PERSONAL BREAKING POINT, ASK FOR HELP. Medicare and Medicaid often pay for medical social services and intermittent home health aide services.

Before pursuing home health services, it's important to find out what kinds and how much of the expense will be covered by Medicare or Medicaid.

Palliative Care Verses Hospice Care

Many people don't know the difference between palliative and hospice care, so if you're confused, don't feel bad. Both are often covered by Medicare, Medicaid, and private insurance. The big difference is that palliative care is used to bring **relief and comfort to patients who may still be pursuing medical treatment**, while hospice is provided for patients who have either **no further medical options for recovery or who have chosen not to pursue further treatment, and have a life expectancy of six months or fewer**.

Care can take place in a home, nursing home, or community living arrangement. Some places also offer hospice treatment in dedicated hospice facilities.

Note that the amount of time per week that hospice provides bedside care is usually limited.

End-of-Life Midwives/Doulas

End-of-life Midwives (or) Doulas are a growing body of trained carers across America that are changing the way the dying are administered to. These doulas focus on normalizing the dying process. Their goal is to:

relieve stress, support the dying and their families, educate, facilitate, mediate, potentially guide through choices such as MAiD or VSED, implement help, create rituals and ceremonies to honor the dying, and aid in the processing of grief.

A doula's goal is to bring the process of dying as close as possible to the vision and wishes of the one who is passing. At the time that this book was written end-of-life midwife care was not covered by Medicare, Medicaid, or most insurance plans.

An end-of-life midwife may offer some, or all, of the following

- **Creation of a safe space** for open and honest communication surrounding impending death

- **Companionship** for the dying

- **Advocacy for the wishes** of the dying person so his or her wishes are respected

- **Education**, offering information about what can and often should be done prior to death regarding paperwork, dying options, the stages of dying, and much more

- **Facilitation** for the competition of tasks such as writing letters to loved ones or organizing legal papers

- **Help in the creation** of memorial projects including the creation of videos, artwork, and journals

- **Organization** of, and sometimes participation in, a living funeral

- **Respite for carers** by sitting with the dying so they can have time for self-care

- **Services that alleviate stress** and sometimes pain such as reiki, guided meditation, essential oils application, and gentle massage

- **Sitting** at the vigil at the bedside of the dying

- **Organization** and sometime officiation at home funerals or traditional funerals

- **Comfort** and resources for those who are grieving

The Vigil

The time immediately preceding death is referred to as the vigil. For the dying, it is a period in which they are actively transitioning from life to death. To be present while this transition happens is to witness the MIRACLE of death.

Many cultures have unique practices during the vigil period. These may include:

final rites, moving the body from the bed to the ground, prayers, cutting of hair, and guided meditations.

As a witness to the period just prior to death, those present should respect rituals that may seem strange based upon their personal religion, culture, and experiences.

Prayer for the Dying

You are surrounded by those who love you.

There is nothing to fear.

We will let nothing harm you.

You are not, and will not, be alone.

We have wrapped you in prayers

And happy memories to keep out the cold.

Our whispers of gratitude for your role
in our lives

Blow across your body to cool your
heated skin.

Our energy joins yours so you may do

What you must do when you must.

We are here to witness an end.

We are here to witness a beginning.

We are here because we are a part of you,

And you are a part of us,

And that bond will never be broken,

Or forgotten.

All is well. All is as it should be.

You are in the slipstream

Of countless numbers of others

Who have prepared a way for you.

We will miss you and that allows us

To release you from our love-bonds,

And rejoice in the idea that
you are ready to **fly free**.

Attending a Vigil

Your job when attending or overseeing a vigil is to offer a peaceful passing surrounded by love. These concepts can help make that happen:

- **Ask people to** identify themselves when entering the room and approaching the bed.

- **Limit the number** of people in the room to maintain a sense of calm.

- **It's believed that hearing** is the last sense to cease so use this time to talk about loving memories.

- **A gentle touch** can speak words.

- **Have a team in place** so those involved can take turns sitting bedside.

- **Bring things needed** for vigil sitters including water, coffee, snacks, lotion, lip balm, a scarf or blanket, a back pillow, and books.

- **Let your loved** one sleep.

- **Keep in touch** with others outside of the vigil room. A communication tree takes the pressure off a single person to share updates.

- **Some believe in verbally** giving the dying permission to pass by saying something like, "It's okay for you to let go now." I modify this message to say, "We will miss you, but we will take care of each other. You will know when it is time to leave, and I'll be here when you do."

The Moment I Left

You flew.
Did you wish to spare me the pain
   of seeing your departure?
Perhaps passing through the veil
   was an experience too intimate to share?
Did saying the final goodbye face-to-face
   seem too painful to bear?
Did the ferocity of my love tether you to life?
Maybe I stretched the tether thin enough
   for you to snap it when I stepped
   into the hall?
No matter.
During this transition
   when so much was out of your control,
   you took control of the ultimate life choice.
You did it your way!
And to that I can merely say,

Amen.

What to Expect During the Vigil

If you are attending a vigil, you're witnessing one of the two most important life events of your loved one's life (birth being the other).

It is awe-inspiring, but may also be scary if you don't know what to expect.

What happens as death comes right up to the foot of the death bed?

Every "dying" is different

Dying is a unique recipe. Here are common ingredients, but not all will be part of every person's last days or hours.

- **Become confused**
- **Try to leave the bed**, saying he or she wants to go home or needs to leave
- **See, and speak** to people not physically in the room
- **Experience brief moments** of lucidity and want to talk
- **Be fatigued** or sleepy
- **Refuse food** and drink
- **Become anxious**
- **Have shortness of breath** or breathe differently
- **Undergo a cooling** of hands, arms, feet, and legs
- **Exhibit changes** in skin color
- **Breathe with a gurgling noise** caused by phlegm in the back of the throat
- **Have glassy** eyes

After Death Must-Do's

After the death of your loved one,

when all you want to do is

go to bed for a year or two

curled into the tightest ball your
body can form,

you must find a way to get back
into a vertical position.

There is work to be done.

LOTS OF WORK.

This list will get you started,

but it is by no means comprehensive.

Get an Official Death Certificate

No death certificate, no funeral. It's as simple as that. If your loved one died at home, call his or her doctor (or 911, if your loved one was not under a doctor's care.) You will need a doctor to verify the death.

If your loved one died under hospice care, in a hospital, or in a nursing home a doctor connected with the facility can declare the death.

As for the official death certificate . . . the funeral home or coroner can supply copies, or you can get them by contacting the Department of Vital Statistics. You will need at least 10 official copies.

Tell Friends and Family

Chances are that many have been waiting for the phone call. You may wish to send a group email or utilize the phone tree you put in place during your loved one's journey toward death.

The Funeral and Burial

With luck, your loved one made clear what he or she wanted to have done with the body. If this is not the case, it's up to the family to decide.

Secure Your Loved One's Home

Clean out the fridge. Water the plants or gift them to others to care for. Rehome pets. Safeguard items of value by locking them away. Collect mail and have future posts forwarded.

Contact Employer

Notify your loved one's employer of the death and find out if there are checks or benefits due.

Find the Will

The will usually identifies the executor for the estate. It will be the executor's job to supervise the tasks of seeing that the estate is settled.

Identify or Hire a Team

A trust and estate attorney are not necessary but will make an executor's job easier, especially if the estate is large or complicated. A CPA will know what taxes must be filed and when.

Make an Inventory and Track Down Assets

Assets may include real estate, personal property, investments, insurance policies, vehicles, banked monies, and more.

Determine What Bills Will Need to Be Paid

Make final payments on outstanding bills and close those accounts.

Close Accounts

Cancel your loved one's phone contract, cable and internet, credit card accounts, utilities, driver's license, insurance policies, email accounts, etc.

Contact and Supply Death Certificates

It is important to contact the Social Security Administration, life insurance companies, banks, credit card agencies (Equifax, Experian, or TransUnion) and the Bureau of Transportation to notify them about the death. Most will require an official copy of the death certificate.

Decide what to do with your loved one's possessions.

In some areas there are companies that specialize in cleaning out homes of the deceased. Reach out for help!

TAKING CARE OF YOURSELF

You are emotionally, and perhaps physically, depleted. The road up to the death of your loved one has called for you to utilize all of your

strength, balance, imagination, fortitude, empathy, wisdom, creativity, kindness, hope, responsibility, authenticity, courage, leadership skills, decisiveness, optimism, honesty, tact, consideration, reliability, faith, innovation, gentleness, intelligence, resilience, optimism, reverence, humor, benevolence, candor, cheerfulness, commitment, compassion, dependability, determination, discipline, endurance, enthusiasm, flexibility, generosity, initiative, integrity, patience, respect, sacrifice, sincerity, strength, trust, understanding, vision, and LOVE .

I Am a Rag

Loved ones say, "This is normal."
They assure me that this weariness,
That feels like a rock on my chest,
With rock-twins tied to my arms and legs,
Will pass.

Time, I'm told, will heal.
I'm told to ask for help
From those who loved my loving,
And watched my journey from life to death
At the side of my loved one.

Right now, I am a slop of a rag.
Web-fragile, full of holes,
Stretched out of shape, wet with tears,
Heavy and limp, not good for much,
Over thinking, over feeling,
Feeling nothing.
Feeling over
Just DONE.

Grief

There is no one way to grieve. Each person does it differently. So, nobody can tell you what is "right" or "wrong" as you experience your sorrow. There are no rules. There is no time frame.

You may be told that there are set stages of grief that you will pass through—denial, anger, bargaining, depression, and acceptance. But that is nonsense. You may skip all but one of those stages or you might experience all of them but in a completely different order. In many ways, grieving is out of your hands. Your mind and heart are in control. While they are figuring it all out, your job is to take care of yourself.

Stages of Grief

~~Denial~~
~~Anger,~~
~~Bargaining,~~
~~Depression,~~
Acceptance

Denial
Anger,
Bargaining,
Depression . . .

Trauma's Effects

Stress and fatigue can lead to all kinds of unpleasant things like

headaches, muscle pain, upset stomachs, and problems sleeping. It can make you unfocused, angry, and anxious.

Your family and friends have their hands full dealing with their own situations. You need to do what you can to take care of yourself.

The Obvious

- **Eating the right foods** can cut levels of cortisol and adrenaline and strengthen the immune system.

- **Eat more complex carbs**, oranges, leafy green vegetables, soybeans, fatty fish, nuts and seeds, avocadoes, and raw vegetables.

- **Drink water**. It lowers stress chemicals in the body.

- **Sleep eight hours a day**. Sleep calms the body, helps concentration, makes it easier to think clearly, and helps stabilize your mood.

- **Exercise. It lowers stress** hormones and stimulates the production of endorphins, which help you feel better physically and emotionally.

- **Seek help** from a good therapist. It's worth both the time and money.

- **Monitor drug** and alcohol use.

Less Obvious Grief Busters

- **Put on your favorite tunes**. Sing and dance until you've released the feelings that have been sitting like a lead weight in your gut. Or pick up a pen and paper and write a song that expresses what's in your heart.

- **Emote those feelings** into a pillow. Scream and howl until you've got no screams left inside you.

- **Create an "emotion box."** Fill it with pictures that reflect your feelings. Tightly close the lid. The emotions will be there if you feel like visiting them, but you don't have to focus on them throughout the day.

- **Journal**. (If you rolled your eyes, I get it. The idea of journaling can seem like homework.) BUT a journal truly can help because by putting things into words you are untangling a ball of feelings and eventually, they will make more sense.

You

Self-care is not self-ish.

End of poem.

- **Adopt a pet**. There is nothing like a four-footed furry ball of love to make you feel less alone.

- **Take a trip** to a place you have always wanted to visit. Travel changes perspective.

- **Volunteer**. Helping others fills up both the giver and the receiver with gratitude.

- **Find a new hobby**, which may sound ridiculous when you are so depleted. But a new hobby can give you something to focus on other than death.

- **Spring clean** because organizing and getting rid of things that you don't need can make you feel lighter. Less stuff translates into less responsibility, and you have enough on your shoulders.

Life Goes On

Because it is worth repeating, I WILL.

There may be minutes, hours, days, weeks, or months when you truly question how you can go on without your loved one. You may tell yourself, "I cannot do this! I cannot bear this!" But you can, and you will.

As all those who have grieved before, you will somehow put one foot in front of the other. Gradually, you will remember how to breathe. The world that became shades of mournful gray will start to shimmer with color. And, when you least expect it, you will open your mouth and a rusty laugh will surprise you by bursting out. Your life will never be the same without the one you love, but you will learn to exist in this new version.

I PROMISE

From the Other Side

White rabbits can be drawn from hats,
And coins plucked from ears.
Babies emerge wailing from wombs.
The deathly ill can heal and rise from
    their beds.
A flower often sprouts where it was
    never planted.
The sound of the sea can be heard in a shell.
A mountain returns your spoken words.
Fog can be seen, but never touched,
And the moon changes shape in the
    night sky.

The world is full of magic

And so I allow myself to believe that

somehow, some way,

Those who come after will sense my presence,

like a voice echoing through time.

They will pause labors or pleasures and

wonder—who?

And as long as I reside in their minds

and hearts,

I will never truly be gone.

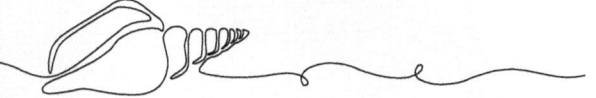

About the Author

Kerry Arquette is a psychotherapist specializing in trauma, death, and dying. She is also a trained and vetted End-of-Life-Midwife, working with the dying and their families to experience the best death possible. She is the co-founder of the Colorado End-of-Life Collaborative and is a sought-after lecturer on the topic of death and dying. In addition, Arquette is the author of dozens of books, including craft titles and award-winning children's picture books. Her most recent book of poetry, *WAR CRIES: UNHEARD VOICES, UNMARKED GRAVES*, offers original stories from the perspectives of those who died, or whose lives changed forever in WW II.

"Dying can be a challenge for both the departing and their loved ones. Many have had little experience supporting their loved ones through one of the most important times of their life—dying. My hope is that this book is both informative and supportive for those walking this imperative path."

Arquette lives in Denver, Colorado, with her husband and at least one cat. She enjoys reading, walking pilgrimages, being with friends and family, and traveling.